Events That Shaped America

The Siege of
the Alamo

Valerie J. Weber and Janet Riehecky

Gareth Stevens Publishing
A WORLD ALMANAC EDUCATION GROUP COMPANY

Please visit our web site at: www.garethstevens.com
For a free color catalog describing Gareth Stevens Publishing's list of high-quality books and multimedia programs, call 1-800-542-2595 (USA) or 1-800-387-3178 (Canada). Gareth Stevens Publishing's fax: (414) 332-3567.

Library of Congress Cataloging-in-Publication Data

Weber, Valerie.
    The siege of the Alamo / by Valerie J. Weber and Janet Riehecky.
        p. cm. — (Events that shaped America)
    Summary: Describes the causes, events, and aftermath of the battle between the Texans and the Mexicans at the Alamo on March 6, 1836.
    Includes bibliographical references and index.
    ISBN 0-8368-3226-4 (lib. bdg.)
    1. Alamo (San Antonio, Tex.)—Siege, 1836—Juvenile literature. [1. Alamo (San Antonio, Tex.)—Siege, 1836. 2. San Antonio (Tex.)—History.] I. Riehecky, Janet, 1953- II. Title. III. Series.
    F390.W375   2002
    976.4'03—dc21   2002021776

This North American edition first published in 2002 by
Gareth Stevens Publishing
A World Almanac Education Group Company
330 West Olive Street, Suite 100
Milwaukee, WI 53212 USA

This edition © 2002 by Gareth Stevens Publishing.

Produced by Discovery Books
Editor: Valerie J. Weber
Designer and page production: Sabine Beaupré
Photo researcher: Sabrina Crewe
Maps and diagrams: Stefan Chabluk
Gareth Stevens editorial direction: Mark J. Sachner
Gareth Stevens art direction: Tammy Gruenewald
Gareth Stevens production: Susan Ashley

Photo credits: Corbis: pp. 5, 10, 15, 18, 24, 27; Daughters of the Republic of Texas Library: p. 22; Granger Collection: cover, p. 6; Library of Congress: p. 8; North Wind Picture Archives: pp. 7, 21; San Antonio Conservation Society: p. 26; Texas Department of Transportation: pp. 9, 20; Texas State Library and Archive Commission: pp. 11, 12, 13, 17, 19, 23, 25.

Printed in the United States of America

1 2 3 4 5 6 7 8 9 06 05 04 03 02

Contents

Introduction

Remember

"Remember the Alamo!" The cry echoes down through American history. Remember a fort where Texan rebels and their American supporters died long ago? Why remember?

In 1836, Texas was part of Mexico, but the government had allowed Americans to settle there. Those Americans brought with them the belief that they should govern themselves, and they **rebelled** against the Mexican government. During this rebellion, the Mexicans surrounded the rebels in the Alamo fort and kept it under **siege** for two weeks.

Until 1821, Mexico and Texas were part of the Spanish Empire in North, South, and Central America. Then Mexico won its independence from Spain. Texas stayed a Mexican **province** until 1836.

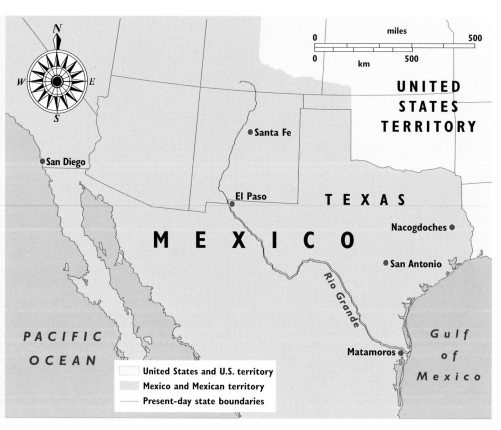

4

The siege ended when, on March 6, 1836, the Mexican army attacked the fort. Within a few hours, nearly everyone inside the fort had been killed.

Two Peoples Clash

Many Mexican soldiers died in that battle as well, fighting to keep Texas part of Mexico. The fight wasn't just about who owned the land or governed the people, however. Americans and Mexicans had different languages, beliefs, and ways of life. Americans brought slaves with them when they settled in Texas. They hoped to become rich by farming huge areas of land using slave labor. Mexico, however, had banned slavery.

A Symbol of Freedom

The Alamo quickly became a symbol of freedom for white Texans and Americans. After the defeat at the Alamo, the rebels became more determined. Mexico was defeated soon after and Texas became a **republic**.

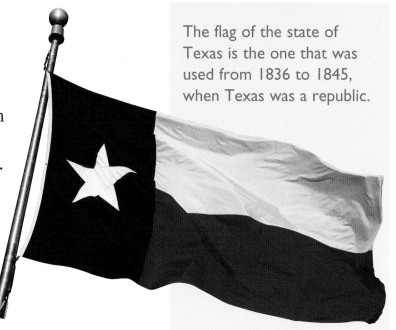

The flag of the state of Texas is the one that was used from 1836 to 1845, when Texas was a republic.

Victory or Death

"To the People of Texas & all Americans in the world:

"I am besieged, by a thousand or more of the Mexicans under Santa Anna . . . The enemy has demanded surrender at discretion, otherwise, the garrison is to be put to the torch, if the fort is taken. I have answered the demand with a cannon shot, and our flag still waves proudly from the walls. I shall never surrender or retreat. Then, I call on you in the name of liberty, of patriotism, and everything dear to the American character, to come to our aid with all dispatch. The enemy . . . will no doubt increase to three or four thousand in four to five days. If this call is neglected I am determined to sustain myself as long as possible & die like a soldier who never forgets what is due his honor and that of his country. Victory or death."

Letter to Texas Governor Henry Smith from William Travis, Alamo defender, February 1836

Chapter One

The People of Texas

The Native Texans

Of course, the land around the Alamo—now located in San Antonio—wasn't always the Mexicans' land. Native peoples had lived there for thousands of years, hunting animals and raising crops such as beans and corn.

The Caddo Indians mostly lived in villages in eastern Texas, although they often made long hunting trips pursuing buffalo for meat and hides. The name for Texas probably comes from the Caddo word *tejas,* meaning "friend." The Spanish people who came later used the word for the entire area. When Americans pronounced the word, they turned it into "Texas."

A Caddo village in Texas is visited by a French explorer named Robert Cavalier de la Salle in the 1680s. The painting is by George Catlin.

Other Native American groups also lived in the area. The Karankawas lived along the Gulf of Mexico, while the Wichitas and Tonkawas stayed further inland, in central Texas. The Coahuiltecans hunted and farmed south of present-day San Antonio. The Lipan people lived in western Texas, where, by the eighteenth century, they frequently warred with the Comanches who had moved into the area.

The Spanish Arrive

When the Spanish came to the **New World**, they were looking for gold. When they found no gold in Texas in the early 1500s, the Spanish left the area. They did not return to Texas for many years.

Gifts of the Spanish: Horses and Smallpox

Spanish explorers brought horses to the Americas, which changed the Native Americans' way of life forever. Hunting and warfare became much easier on horseback, and with better hunting came better food.

Not all the Spanish gifts were as welcome as the horses, however. The Spanish carried diseases that the Native Americans could not resist. Thousands of people, sometimes entire villages, became ill from smallpox, measles, or influenza and died.

The Spanish came on horseback in the 1500s to search for gold.

The Alamo's Beginnings

In 1718, a Spanish priest, Antonio Olivares, built a tiny **mission**, not much more than a straw hut, near the San Antonio River. Along with other priests in Texas, he hoped to **convert** the Native people to Christianity. The Spanish army also built a military post nearby and a small town across the river. They named the town San Antonio de Béxar, but most people called it just Béxar. Today, the city is called San Antonio.

Six years later, the Spanish began expanding the mission, making a more permanent structure. They built a rectangular wall surrounding a large courtyard. The wall would make the mission easier to defend from Indian attacks. Through

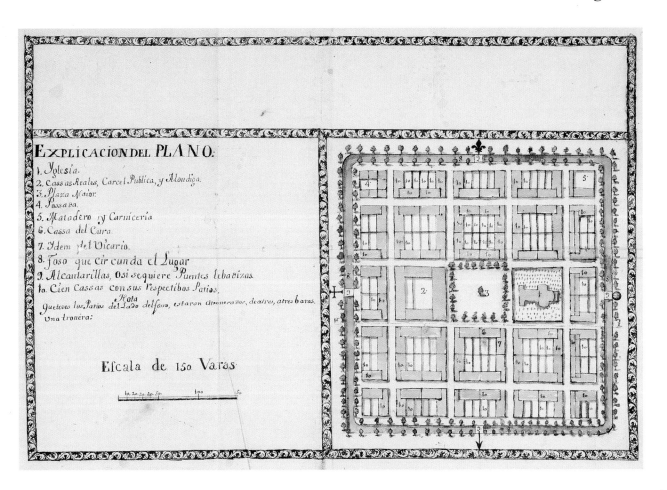

8

the center, water from the San Antonio River flowed in a large ditch. There were storerooms, workshops, and housing. By 1758, a church stood at the courtyard's eastern edge.

The Alamo Becomes a Military Post

During the 1700s, the town of Béxar gained people, but the mission did not. Native Americans saw no reason to change their religious beliefs. By the end of the century, the Spanish had closed all their Texan missions.

In 1801, however, the Spanish returned to Béxar to use the mission as a military post. They added more walls and turned some of the housing into **barracks**. The soldiers who lived there renamed the mission the *Alamo*, Spanish for "cottonwood tree," after their last post in Mexico.

Surrounded by cottonwoods and other trees, the Alamo church, built in 1758, still stands today. The U.S. army added the parapet, the low wall on top, in the 1840s.

9

The Mexicans Rebel

Spain still ruled Mexico at this time. The Spanish had wealth and power; the Mexican Indians had nothing. In 1810, Miguel Hidalgo y Costilla, a priest, urged the Mexicans to rebel against their Spanish rulers. He wanted an end to slavery and to Spanish taxes on Mexico. The Spanish killed Hidalgo a year later, but the seeds of rebellion had been sown. The struggle continued.

Spain sent General Agustín de Iturbide to Mexico to fight the rebels. He changed sides, however, led the Mexicans to victory over the Spanish, and then proclaimed himself emperor. Now Mexico was free, and Texas became a Mexican province instead of a Spanish colony.

Iturbide did not last long as Mexico's ruler. In 1824, the country became a republic. Military leaders struggled with each other to take over the government, and no one stayed leader for long. In 1833, General Antonio López de Santa Anna declared himself president of Mexico.

American Settlers Arrive in Texas

During the early 1800s, American **colonists** flooded westward out of the original thirteen colonies. They took land from Native American peoples and claimed it as their own. Many Americans felt the United States should expand its boundaries all the way to the Pacific Ocean. In fact, the U.S. government offered to buy Texas from Spain but was refused.

Moses Austin, a miner, thought of another way Americans could get land in Texas. Just before Mexico split from Spain, he asked the Spanish government if he could bring white American families (often called Anglo-Americans or Anglos) to settle in Texas. The government agreed, but said that the settlers must be loyal to Spain, not to the United States. Another condition was that the settlers become Catholic, as the Spanish people were, but this rule was never enforced.

Moses Austin died before any settlers arrived. But in 1821, his son Stephen started bringing colonists to Texas under an agreement with the new Mexican rulers. By 1825, Austin's colony had 1,350 Anglos and 450 African-American slaves.

Antonio López de Santa Anna (1794–1876)

Antonio López de Santa Anna was born into a wealthy and powerful Spanish family in Mexico. He helped push Iturbide out of power, then grabbed control of Mexico for himself. Santa Anna was forced from the presidency several times and fled to Cuba and Jamaica. In 1853, he became president of Mexico for the last time; two years later, he was forced out again. Santa Anna died penniless in 1876.

Chapter Two

The Texans Rebel

General Martín Perfecto de Cós was President Santa Anna's brother-in-law. Santa Anna sent him to Texas to crush the Anglo rebels.

More Texans than Mexicans

Austin was not the only person bringing settlers to Texas. During the 1820s, the Mexican government allowed others to bring settlers as well. Thousands of Americans streamed into Texas.

By the early 1830s, over thirty thousand Anglos lived in Texas, outnumbering the Mexican and Native people. Most lived in the east, far from the older Mexican towns, but some moved into Mexican areas. A few Anglos settled in Béxar.

Governing the Anglos

During the 1820s, the government in Mexico paid little attention to the Texans; it expected the settlers to govern themselves. The settlers did, but not as the government had hoped. They ignored many Mexican laws, grabbing huge areas of land and **smuggling** goods into the area. They did

Americanizing Texas

"I wish a great immigration this fall and winter from Kentucky, Tennessee, everywhere, . . . anyhow. For fourteen years I have had a hard time of it, but nothing shall daunt my courage nor abate my exertions to Americanize Texas."

Stephen Austin in a letter
to his cousin Mary Austin Holley, 1835

not pay taxes to the Mexican government, as people in other provinces did. They also held slaves, which was against Mexican law.

In 1830, the Mexican government tightened the laws in Texas. It forbade more settlers from coming in, banned future slavery, and demanded that Texans pay their taxes and stop smuggling.

The Anglos hated the new restrictions. While they were grateful to Mexico for their cheap land and had promised to obey the government, they believed in American ideals and rights, especially the right for American men to have a voice in government. When General Santa Anna became president in 1833, both Anglos and Mexicans lost many rights.

Santa Anna's rule split the Anglo settlers. Some, called the "peace party," were willing to remain loyal to Mexico as long as they could keep their land, slaves, and the rights they used to have. Other Anglos, especially those who had not received land, were ready to split from Mexico and join the United States. They were known as the "war party."

W.B. Travis By Wiley Martin Dec. 1835

William Barret Travis arrived in Texas in 1831 and soon joined the Texas "war party." In his final battle, he commanded the Alamo, where he died in 1836.

The Fighting Begins

By June 1835, the war party was ready for a fight. Mexican government agents were pushing Anglos to pay taxes, and Mexican soldiers, led by General Martín Perfecto de Cós, were coming into their province and others nearby to break up local governments.

Against the peace party's wishes, the war party, armed with a cannon and led by William Barret Travis, went off to capture the Mexican fort at Anahuác. The local military leader **surrendered** without a fight.

General Cós Responds

A furious Cós demanded the Texans hand over the rebels, but now both Anglo parties joined together against him.

In response, General Cós brought hundreds of soldiers into Texas, making his headquarters at Béxar. The soldiers took weapons from the Texans and demanded the cannon from the Anglo village of Gonzales. The men of Gonzales, backed by the rebels, refused. A small fight followed, with the first shots fired in the war for Texas freedom. The result: the Texans kept both the cannon and the village.

The Siege of Béxar

After the victory at Gonzales, not just Texans but Americans **rallied** to Austin when he called for support. American volunteers poured into Texas to join the rebels, who were forming their own army.

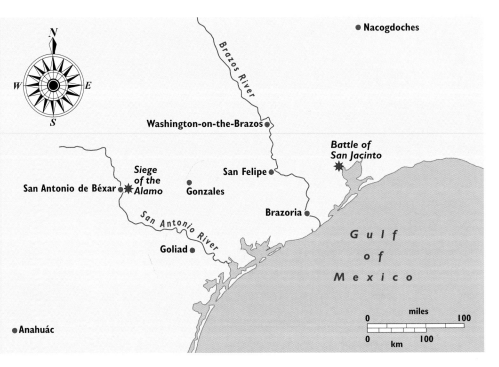

This map shows the towns of Gonzales, Goliad, Anahuác, and San Felipe, all places where Texans rebelled against Mexico.

Austin was made a general of the rebel army and led the volunteers and Texans in an attack on the Mexican headquarters at Béxar. By late October 1835, about five hundred Texans and American volunteers had surrounded the Mexican army in a siege of Béxar and the town's old fort, the Alamo. The siege continued for many weeks.

A Rebel Government

In November, meanwhile, a group of fifty-seven Texans, meeting at San Felipe, wrote "A Declaration of Causes," calling for a **revolution** against the Mexican government. They also set up an independent government. Henry Smith was chosen as governor. Sam Houston, who had recently come from Tennessee, was made commander of the Texan rebel army. Some Mexicans were also against Santa Anna, but most of the four thousand Mexicans in Texas were either against the rebellion or stayed out of the fight altogether.

Sam Houston in the 1850s, when he was a United States senator for Texas. He had been governor of Tennessee and later became governor of Texas.

Texans Take the Alamo

On December 5, 1835, the Texan army finally attacked Béxar and the Mexicans surrendered four days later. An angry Santa Anna gathered a large army to take to Texas.

The Texan army was divided. Some of the soldiers left with supplies and weapons from the Alamo, preparing to take their fight into Mexico itself. Colonel James Neill was left in charge of Béxar with about one hundred men, mostly American volunteers. Neill moved into the Alamo, begging General Houston for supplies and more men.

Decisions

Houston knew the Mexicans had not given up the Alamo for good; they would return, but when? Which positions could the Texans defend from the Mexicans? Decisions had to be made.

Houston sent Colonel James Bowie, a colorful Texan adventurer, with about thirty men to decide whether to defend the Alamo. Houston expected Bowie would move the men out of the fort and destroy it so the Mexicans could not move back in. Bowie, however, did just the opposite. He decided that the rebel Texans should hold onto the Alamo and **fortify** it. Then they could use it as a base from which to fight against the Mexican army.

In 1836, the Alamo church was almost in ruins. The Texans put up wooden posts to make a palisade that closed the gap between the church and the wall around the Alamo. To mount their cannons, they built dirt platforms.

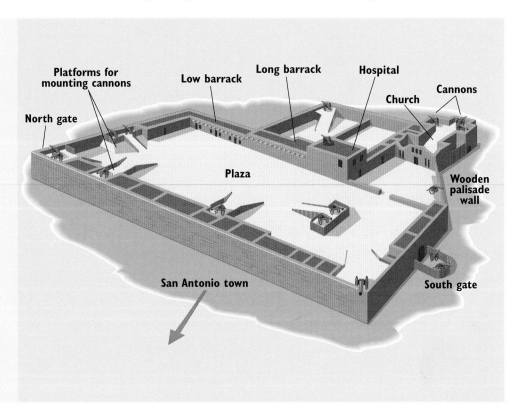

Platforms for mounting cannons · Low barrack · Long barrack · Hospital · Church · Cannons · North gate · Plaza · Wooden palisade wall · San Antonio town · South gate

Chapter Three

The Alamo Surrounded

Into the Fort

Once Bowie had decided to defend the Alamo, Governor Smith sent Lieutenant Colonel William Travis and thirty men to help him. On February 11, 1836, Colonel Neill left Travis in charge of the Texan soldiers.

Davy Crockett, a skilled hunter and teller of tall tales—especially about himself—arrived with twelve **sharpshooters**. Other volunteers, ranging in age from sixteen to fifty-seven, also arrived. They came from all over the United States and other countries. Many were hunters and fur trappers. The volunteers came for many reasons: to get land promised by the rebel government in exchange for help, to battle for freedom, or simply to join in the fight. The volunteers chose Bowie as their leader, and so now there were two leaders in the Alamo.

Bowie and Travis argued over who was in charge, even as they tried to make the Alamo stronger together. They also asked for soldiers and supplies from General Houston and Governor Smith. None came. Meanwhile, Santa Anna and his soldiers marched closer every day.

In 1828, Davy Crockett left his home in Tennessee for Texas, where he hoped to become rich.

This bronze plaque at the Alamo shows Texan soldiers and volunteers heading for the Alamo. Many volunteers were excellent hunters and sharpshooters.

Travis ordered all the soldiers from Béxar into the Alamo; they took food from houses in the town since few supplies had been kept at the fort. Men from the town joined them, along with between fifteen and twenty-five women and children. Again the call went out to the rebel army and government for help.

No Mercy

On February 23, 1836, Santa Anna arrived in Béxar. Hundreds of his men, armed and supplied, were ready for the fight. They raised a blood red flag with a skull and crossbones, showing they would neither give mercy nor expect it. The siege of the Alamo had begun. When Travis and Bowie asked to talk, Santa Anna said they would have to surrender immediately, without any promises that their lives or their men's would be spared. This the Texans refused to do. In response to the flag, they fired a cannon.

Inside the Alamo

A day later, James Bowie, who had been gravely ill for weeks, put Travis in charge of all the volunteers. Santa Anna's men surrounded the fort, but even so men managed to slip in and out of the Alamo to fetch supplies and carry messages. Thirty-two men from Gonzales got through to the Alamo as well. At any time, men could have abandoned the fight and the fort, but they chose to stay.

Inside the Alamo, the situation was bad. A quickly dug well provided little water; not enough wood remained for fires to warm the Texans in the bitter cold. Outside, Santa Anna's army grew to two thousand men.

Declaration of Independence

In Washington-on-the-Brazos, an Anglo town, the rebel government wrote the Texas Declaration of Independence. It was passed on March 2, 1836. According to the declaration, the Mexican government had "ceased to protect the lives, liberty, and property of the people." Because of this, the people had the right "to take their political affairs into their own hands."

The Texan rebels wanted four rights from the government of Mexico: their own representatives in the Mexican government; their own armies and weapons; religious freedom; and the right to own slaves. The Declaration stated that people who were slaves now would remain slaves forever. Somehow, these white men saw nothing wrong in claiming freedom for themselves while denying it to their African-American slaves.

With the Declaration of Independence, the Texans publicly declared they wanted to be independent, not just get their rights back from the Mexican government.

Chapter Four

The Battle

On March 6, 1836, several hundred Mexican soldiers gathered in the dark around the Alamo.

While the Alamo Slept

It was still dark on March 6, 1836, when Santa Anna ordered his men awake. Silently, the soldiers stole away from their tents to surround the walls of the Alamo. They had awaited this moment for two weeks, keeping the fort under siege with cannon fire. Now it was time for a full attack.

The Mexican Army Attacks

Just before dawn, the final fight began. The Mexicans charged at the fort. The Texans inside were surprised by the assault. Many were sick and exhausted, but they dragged themselves to positions on the four walls of the fort.

Santa Anna's first line of soldiers, cut down by the Alamo's sharpshooters, never made it to the fort. The Mexican leader sent more men to their deaths, and wave after wave of soldiers tried to climb the fort's walls. Finally, the army retreated into the town to regroup.

Then they tried again. Brave Mexicans climbed the walls, urged on by their officers. Soon the fort swarmed with soldiers. The Texans were outnumbered. They fought back fiercely, but they were nearly all killed in the battle.

The Alamo Falls

The rest took **refuge** in the buildings on the east wall. Those in the long barrack continued to fight bravely, knowing little hope remained. Others hid in the church, but they, too, were found and killed. Although some Texans tried to surrender, they were shot. Too sick to rise, Jim Bowie was shot in his bed.

Between 6:30 and 9:00 A.M., the battle ended. Some men who had been taken prisoner were then executed. Only a few who had been inside the fort remained alive, including Travis's slave Joe, two men who had escaped, a few women, and some of the children.

What Really Happened?

Because the stories told by the survivors and Mexican soldiers varied so much, no one knows for sure how many died at the Alamo. Estimates range from 190 to 260 rebels and 400 to 500 Mexicans. Another 200 or more Mexicans were wounded.

In Mexican stories about the Alamo, defenders of the fort were called "the devil Texans." To Americans, however, they would become heroes.

Cannon fire filled the air with flames and smoke as the Mexicans climbed the walls with their ladders.

Chapter Five

Remember the Alamo

Susanna Dickinson and her one-year-old daughter Angelina were among the few to survive inside the Alamo.

The Story Grows

After the battle, Santa Anna heard that Susanna Dickinson, an Anglo, had survived the fight at the Alamo. He sent her to warn General Sam Houston and the Texans to stop their rebellion or suffer the same fate as the defenders of the Alamo.

The story changed as it spread. When first questioned, Dickinson and Travis's slave Joe said they had both hidden during the battle and seen little. They changed their story over time, however, adding details to events they now claimed to have seen. There was no question, though, that many men had died at the Alamo. Americans and Texans wanted revenge.

Death in Goliad

Seeing that Santa Anna was set on punishing the rebels, Houston ordered Colonel James Fannin to abandon Goliad and its fort. The Mexican army neared. Fannin finally led several hundred men out of town on March 19, 1836. When the Mexicans chased him, he turned and fought but surrendered the next day.

Santa Anna Explains

"[The stubbornness] of Travis and his soldiers was the cause of the death of the whole of them, for not one would surrender. The struggle lasted more than two hours, and until the **ramparts** were resolutely scaled by Mexican soldiers."

Letter from Santa Anna to painter and historian Henry Arthur McArdle in Independence, Texas, March 19, 1874

Mexican soldiers shooting the Texan and American prisoners at Goliad. A few Mexicans managed to hide some of the prisoners, saving their lives.

The Mexicans took over four hundred Texan soldiers prisoner, including a group of eighty-two new volunteers from New York. Santa Anna ordered them all killed. A few Texan soldiers escaped, and the New Yorkers were spared, along with some American doctors. All the rest died in the gunfire.

Santa Anna Sweeps through Mexico

After his victories at the Alamo and Goliad, Santa Anna wanted to get rid of all the Americans in Texas. His army moved eastward, toward the U.S. border. Thousands of Anglo families—women, children, and the elderly—fled ahead of the army, leaving their homes to be destroyed.

The Texan men, however, were **enraged** by all the killings. They joined General Houston's army, which had grown to about fourteen hundred, retreating from Santa Anna. Houston's newest men need training. While they were retreating, he taught them to be soldiers. Few understood Houston's plans, and many accused him of being afraid to stand and fight.

Stand Up and Fight
"Sir. The enemy are laughing you to scorn. You must fight them. You must retreat no further. The country expects you to fight. The salvation of the country depends on your doing so."

Letter from Texas president David G. Burnet to General Sam Houston, April 1836

This painting of Sam Houston by Seymour Thomas shows the general leading his men to the Battle of San Jacinto.

On the San Jacinto Plain

By April 19, 1836, the Mexican army had pushed Houston and his men onto the San Jacinto plain. When General Cós and his soldiers arrived that night, the Mexican army grew to about twelve hundred men, all badly tired.

Frustrated by retreating, Houston's men demanded an immediate fight. On April 21, the general led his soldiers against Santa Anna's army, catching it completely unprepared. As Houston's men ran forward, Colonel Sidney Sherman yelled, "Remember the Alamo!" Eighteen minutes later, 630 Mexican soldiers were dead, 200 more wounded, and 730 taken prisoner. Only 9 Texan soldiers had died.

Santa Anna was caught the next day. Although the American soldiers wanted Santa Anna killed, Houston told him he would be spared if he took his army out of Texas and agreed to the province's independence. Santa Anna agreed.

Texan Independence

Because Santa Anna had been forced into this agreement, the Mexican government refused to honor it. That made no difference to the Texans, who declared themselves free and elected Houston president of the new Republic of Texas.

Texans wanted their state to become part of the United States right away, but the U.S. government wanted Texans to form their own government first. However, the United States and many European nations did recognize Texas as a nation.

After the Battle of San Jacinto, Santa Anna (center left, in white pants) was brought before a wounded Sam Houston lying under the tree.

The United States admitted Texas to the Union on December 29, 1845. Mexico immediately broke off relations with the United States, and the two countries went to war in 1846. Mexico surrendered to the United States in 1848, and the border of Texas was set along the Rio Grande. As part of the treaty ending the war, the Mexicans also sold today's California, Nevada, Utah, and parts of Arizona, New Mexico, Colorado, and Wyoming to the United States for $15 million.

The Problem of Slavery

Texas might have been a U.S. state much earlier if it hadn't insisted on the right for white people to own slaves. In 1844, the same number of states allowed slavery as the number of states that did not. Letting Texas join the United States as a slave state would upset that balance. Within a year, the states without slavery allowed Texas to join. The problem of slavery, however, would not go away and led to the Civil War in 1861.

Conclusion

In 1898, when this photograph was taken, a department store had been built where the Alamo's barracks and other housing once stood.

What Became of the Alamo?

After all those deaths, Mexico kept the Alamo for only two months before the Texans returned on June 4, 1836. Over the next forty years, the Alamo was used to store military supplies, to house Confederate Army soldiers during the Civil War, and as a general store and warehouse. A bar, a restaurant, and a meat market followed.

Texans thought all this business activity showed a lack of respect for an important site. In 1883, the State of Texas bought the Alamo church but not the businesses. Twenty years later, a group called the Daughters of the Republic of Texas began raising money to buy the Alamo. Clara Driscoll's grandfathers had fought at San Jacinto; remembering them, she bought the entire site and donated it to the state in 1905.

You can still visit the Alamo. The Daughters of the Republic of Texas take care of the church and fort remains for the more than 2.5 million visitors yearly. Exhibits explain its history from its earliest beginnings to today.

Looking Back

As often happens, the stories people told of the Alamo and what happened there became more important than the facts. The Texans and Americans had many reasons to fight for the Alamo, including wanting to become rich landowners and to keep their slaves. However, most believed in the fight for freedom, and that became the only reason that people in Texas and the rest of United States wanted to hear. No one can argue about the courage of the Alamo's defenders, however, and stories about that courage are still told.

Today the Alamo church and grounds stand in the middle of busy San Antonio, previously the small town of Béxar.

Time Line

1718   Mission San Antonio de Valero is built near the San Antonio River.

1724   Mission built on site of today's Alamo.

1793   Spanish close the mission.

1801   Spanish soldiers change Mission San Antonio de Valero into a military base and change its name to the Alamo.

1820   Moses Austin gets permission from Spanish to bring settlers to Texas.

1821   Mexico gains its independence from Spain.

1824   Mexico becomes a republic.

1833   Antonio López de Santa Anna becomes president of Mexico.

1835   October 2: Backed by Texan rebels, village of Gonzales refuses to give up cannon to Mexican soldiers.
November: Texans set up rebel government.
December 5–10: Texans attack General Martín Perfecto de Cós and take control of the Alamo.

1836   February 23: General Santa Anna's army arrives outside San Antonio and begins siege.
March 2: Texas declares itself independent of Mexico.
March 6: Santa Anna's army attacks and captures the Alamo.
April 21: General Sam Houston's army defeats Santa Anna's at Battle of San Jacinto.
July: New Republic of Texas elects Sam Houston as its first president.

1845   United States admits Texas as its twenty-eighth state.

1846   United States declares war on Mexico.

1848   Treaty of Guadalupe Hidalgo ends Mexican-American War and gives large areas of Mexican territory to the United States.

1876   Part of Alamo site is turned into a general store.

1883   State of Texas buys Alamo church.

1905   Clara Driscoll gives the entire Alamo site to Texas.

Things to Think About and Do

You Are There

Imagine you are a Texan rebel standing in the Alamo on March 5, 1836. You can hear the Mexican soldiers from their camp, and you've felt the thud of the occasional cannonball. Write two paragraphs describing your surroundings and your feelings, knowing you are about to be attacked. Then imagine you are a Mexican foot soldier knowing you have to climb the walls of the Alamo. Describe your surroundings and your feelings.

Two Views of the Alamo

Draw a picture of the Alamo as you think it might have looked at its very beginnings and another picture of the fight over the Alamo.

A Right to Rebel?

Do you think the Texans were right to rebel against the Mexican government? After all, they had come to settle on Mexican land and had promised to follow Mexico's laws. What do you think about their reasons for rebelling, especially their desire to keep slaves? Write a short paragraph explaining what you think.

Glossary

barrack: housing for soldiers.

colonist: person who lives in a colony, which is an area owned or controlled by another nation.

convert: cause a person to change a belief, usually a religious one.

enraged: deeply angered.

fortify: make stronger.

mission: center built by Spanish in the American Southwest to convert Native Americans to Christianity and exploit their labor.

New World: name for North and South America used by the first Europeans who traveled and settled there. They thought of themselves as from the "Old World."

province: division of a country, like a state in the United States.

rally: come to the support of a person or cause.

rampart: high, broad mound of earth or stone surrounding a guarded place.

rebel: fight against a person or group in power.

refuge: shelter.

republic: nation led by a leader or group of officials elected by the citizens.

retreat: draw back from a battle.

revolution: overthrowing of a government and setting up of a new system of government.

sharpshooter: someone who is highly skilled at shooting a gun.

siege: surrounding of and often attacking an enemy for a long time while cutting off the enemy's food and other supplies. An army puts an enemy's position under siege to force it to surrender.

smuggle: take in and out of a country secretly and against the law.

surrender: give up.

Further Information

Books

Alter, Judy. *Sam Houston: A Leader for Texas* (*Community Builders*). Children's Press, 1998.

Burgan, Michael. *The Alamo* (*We the People*). Compass Point Books, 2001.

Garland, Sherry. *Voices of the Alamo*. Scholastic Press, 2000.

Johnston, Marianne. *Jim Bowie* (*American Legends*). Powerkids Press, 2001.

Love, D. Anne. *I Remember the Alamo*. Yearling Books, 2001.

O'Brien, Steven, Rodolfo Cardona, and James D. Cockcroft. *Antonio López de Santa Anna* (*Hispanics of Achievement*). Chelsea House, 1993.

Santella, Andrew. *The Battle of the Alamo* (*Cornerstones of Freedom*). Children's Press, 1997.

Sita, Lisa. *Indians of the Southwest: Traditions, History, Legends, and Life.* Gareth Stevens, 2001.

Web Sites

www.bchm.org Brazoria County Historical Museum offers exhibits about Stephen Austin's colony that show life as an Anglo settler in Texas.

www.thealamo.org Visitor information, history, and a virtual tour of the Alamo site.

tqjunior.thinkquest.org/3548/index.html A kid-created web site on the Alamo's history and battle; includes links to other sites.

Useful Addresses

The Alamo
300 Alamo Plaza
San Antonio, TX 78299
Telephone: (210) 225-1391

Index